Written by Christine Lazier
Illustrated by Claude and Denise Millet

Specialist advisers:
Dr Jane Mainwaring,
The British Museum (Natural History),
Harry Hope, Agricultural Adviser

ISBN 1 85103 041 7
First published 1988 in the United Kingdom by
Moonlight Publishing Ltd,
131 Kensington Church Street, London W8

POCKET • WORLDS

Cows and Their Cousins

The cows that you see in the fields seem peaceful enough...

The cows that we are used to are gentle grazing animals. But **the cow's ancestor, the aurochs, was a very wild animal indeed!**
Prehistoric men used to hunt it, with only sharpened flints as weapons. They ate the aurochs' meat and the marrow of their bones. They painted pictures of aurochs on the walls of their caves,

This painting of an aurochs is over 15000 years old.

as part of their magic. About six thousand years ago, people began to keep the aurochs in pens so that they were always ready to hand: gradually they became domestic animals that men could turn to for milk and meat.

Highland cattle look a little like pocket-size aurochs.

Look at this cow. She has a tail that she can whisk, and ears that she can twitch, to keep away flies. On her forehead are two short, curved horns. A cow who has not yet had a calf is called a heifer.

Cows usually have one calf a year.

A calf has no horns, only two bumps on its forehead.

Like a human baby, a calf grows inside its mother for nine months before it is born. Shortly before the birth, the cow's udder fills with milk to feed her calf. Cows are mammals; this is the name given to animals which feed their babies on milk.

Cows eat grass, but they also like cereals, beetroot, soya beans . . .

In summer cows live out of doors. **They eat a lot of grass: nearly sixty kilos a day.**

But look out: if grass is scarce and they eat oak leaves or acorns, bracken, meadow-saffron, yew or rape, they may die.

Grass is very hard to digest. The cow has a special way of coping. First she pulls up the grass with her rough tongue and gives it a quick chew. Then she swallows. Later, when she is resting, the pieces of food come back into her mouth to be chewed again slowly and thoroughly with her flat teeth. This is called chewing the cud, or ruminating.

Cows need salt. This is a salt lick.

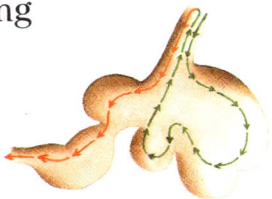

The grass passes through four stomachs.

In winter, most cows live inside. In times past, the cowshed used to be part of the farmhouse. This made it easy to look after the animals in bad winter weather and the heat from the animals' bodies helped to keep the farmer and his family warm.

Nowadays, cows live in special modern cowsheds or in barns which sometimes open out on to yards or fields.

Cows must be milked morning and night. This used to be done by hand, but now farmers use milking machines, which can milk several animals at once. Cows are only milked after calves have been weaned.

A cow may give between 20 and 30 litres of milk each day.

In Alpine countries, cows graze on the open pasture in spring and summer. Meadows with clover and other wild flowers help the cows produce rich, creamy milk.

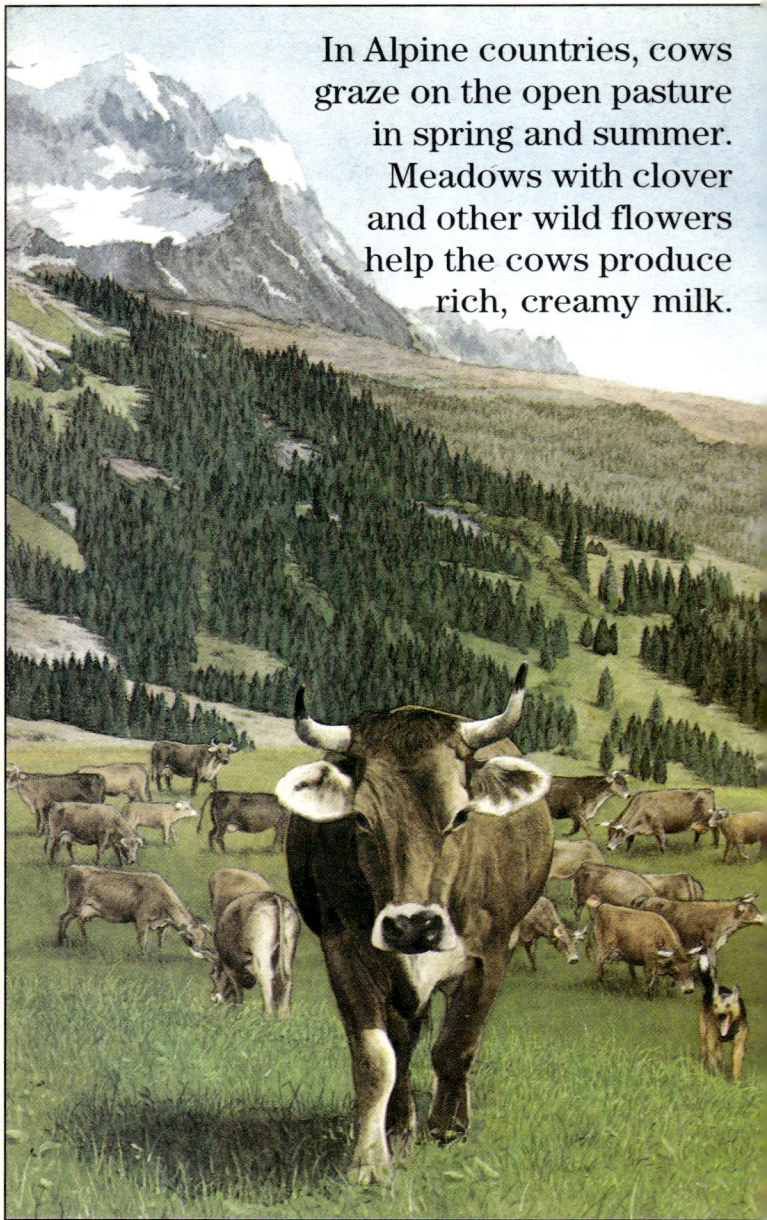

<u>Herds are highly organised.</u> Each herd has a leader who has reached her position by bullying the other cows. The leader is often the strongest and oldest of the cows. Every cow learns to know her place, right down to the weakest and most timid, who has to make way for all the others.

In some parts of southern and eastern Europe you can still see carts pulled by oxen.

These oxen, in China, are pulling along the plough as it breaks up the ground.

In the West Indies, oxen pull the carts which take the sugar-cane from the fields to the factory.

Oxen at work

Oxen, or bullocks, are bulls who have had an operation when they were about a year old. The operation means that, unlike bulls, they can never father a calf. It makes them quieter and easier to handle. For thousands of years, people have used oxen to help them with heavy work like ploughing and pulling carts. Nowadays, in most places, oxen have been replaced by tractors.

Two oxen are often fastened together with a yoke.

Once an ox has been trained, which takes about two years, it can work up to ten hours a day without stopping. Oxen are patient, steady and very strong.

Old-fashioned yokes

Most cows are kept for their milk;
these are dairy cows. Some cows are
used for meat as well, but usually
meat cattle are bullocks.

Jersey (milk)

Kerry (milk)

German Yellow (beef)

Simmental (beef and milk)

Aberdeen Angus (beef)

West Highland (mainly beef)

Finn Cattle (milk)

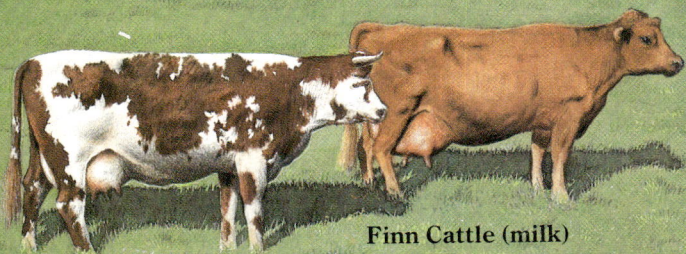

Normande (milk)

Meuse Rein Issel (milk)

Breton Pie noire (milk)

Hereford (beef)

Charolais (beef)

An untreated skin

A tanned skin

What are your shoes made of?

Probably leather from cowskin. For thousands of years, people have made all sorts of things from leather: shoes, clothes, belts, bags.

How do you turn skins into leather?

First, you singe off the hairs and the bits of meat and fat. Then the two layers of skin are separated: the top one is for fine leather, the bottom layer is coarser. Finally, the skins are tanned to make them supple. Then they are dyed.

Natural leather is a light brown colour, but it can be dyed any colour of the rainbow.

Milk is very good for you.

The calcium it contains strengthens your bones and your teeth. The carbohydrates build you up and give you energy. Milk also has essential vitamins. You can drink milk, or eat it as butter, cheese or yoghurt...

What is beef?

It is the meat from cows, bullocks or young bulls. You can eat almost every part of the animals except the soles of their feet! The best meat comes from the backs of young animals. Beef gives you proteins to build up your muscles.

Sirloin

Chump chops

Steak

Hamburger

Rib roast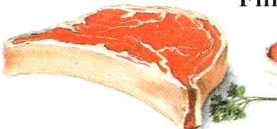

Fillet

Rib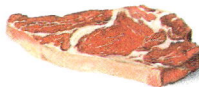

Veal

Cowboys

In the United States cows, bulls and bullocks live almost wild on the ranches. Cowboys on horseback look after them. If an animal strays, they catch it

The mark of the ranch they belong to is burned on to the calves' hide with a hot branding-iron.

with a lasso. The herds tend to be quite lively and adventurous. Riding herd is hard and dusty work – the cowboys wear scarves to cover their mouths and noses when the dust is really bad.

'Ride him, cowboy!'

During rodeos, cowboys try to ride a wild steer, using only one hand, and with just a rope to hold on to. They usually fall off after a few seconds! Rodeo workers dressed as clowns distract the bull while the rider scrambles away.

Yaks aren't afraid of heights, and thanks to their long hair, they don't feel the cold in the high mountains of Central Asia, where they and the Tibetans live. The yaks climb tirelessly

Spinning yak hair

up and down mountains, carrying heavy loads. Yaks give the Tibetans all they need to live on. The Tibetans drink yaks' milk, eat yak meat, make ropes with the hair, clothes, shoes and bags with the leather. They even make bracelets from yak hair twisted with silver.

The Tibetans use dried yak-dung to fuel their fires.

Why are Asian buffalo called water-buffalo? Because they love plunging up to their necks in water. Their gentle natures make them easy to train. They pull carts and work in the wet paddy-fields where rice is grown.

The African buffalo, less gentle than the Asian, paws the ground when it is angry.

African buffalo love wallowing in mud to cool themselves and to get rid of insects.

African buffalo live wild on the African plains. They are very strong and quick-moving, and can be quite savage if they are wounded or scared. Their only enemies are lions and people.

Zebu have been domesticated for over 5000 years. They live in the hot countries of Asia and Africa. Unlike other humped cattle, the humps on their backs do not contain any bone, they

The zebu

are made entirely of fat and muscle, and provide a food-store for the zebu when times are hard. Some zebu have horns over a metre long.

In summer, the males fight to decide who will mate with the females.

There used to be huge herds of bison in North America. Once, there were about 50 million of them roaming the continent. These huge, quick-footed animals were precious to the Indians, who hunted them for their meat, fat, skin, fur...

But when the white men arrived with their guns and their steam trains, they settled on the Indian lands and slaughtered the bison the Indians depended on. Nowadays there are only a few thousand left in wildlife reserves. There used to be bison in Europe too. European bison were not as big as the American bison, and were less wild. They lived in woods and forests. There are still a few left in Poland.

European bison

The **kuri**
lives in Africa.
Its huge horns
are porous, with air
inside them, so that
they do not become too
heavy. The people round
Lake Chad keep kuri for milk and meat.
**To the Masai in East Africa, cattle are
their most important possessions.**
Cattle to them are like money to us. They
trade with them, and how many cattle they
have shows how important they are. The
tribesmen have over 700 different words to
describe their cattle. Even the dung the
cattle leave provides them with fuel for
their fires and material to build their
houses.

Masai boys look after the herds.

In the jungles of Asia lives the fierce **gaur.** Gaur are as big as bison and far more dangerous than lions or tigers.

The gaur

The fastest cows in the world are a cross between a zebu and a **banteng.**

They can run at 70 kilometres an hour. Banteng come from Indonesia, and are the closest living relatives of the aurochs.

The banteng

The **musk-ox** from North America looks a bit like a yak. Its thick fur protects it from the bitter weather and wild storms of the far north where it lives.

During the mating season, the male musk-ox has a very strong scent.

31

A corrida is a battle between a toreador, or
bullfighter, and a bull. In France, the bull
lives to fight another day – in Spain, the bull
is killed.

Spanish fighting bulls are raised in special herds which are kept wild. Wherever you are though, watch out for bulls in fields. They are never to be trusted and may attack you!

Bulls and gods

In ancient Egypt, the sacred bull Apis was worshipped as a god. When one bull died, it was mummified and another was chosen to take its place in the temple, where it was pampered like a prince.

Apis

Cretan bull-dance

The Greeks and the Cretans often painted pictures of the gods riding on bulls, the symbols of power and strength.

Even today, the Swiss decorate their cattle with flowers to celebrate their return to the valleys after their long summer in the mountains. The leader wears the biggest, noisiest bell.

In India, cows are sacred.
They walk through the streets
wherever they want to go, and no one will
hurt them or eat them. There are even
special hospitals for them if they get ill.

Whether for milk or meat, or for help
pulling heavy weights, throughout the ages,
people all over the world have depended
upon the gentle cow and its many cousins.

Index

Pocket Worlds — building up into a child's first encyclopaedia: